# YOU DESERVE
# THE LOVE OF GOD

STEPHEN HILL

©2020

*'You Deserve the Love of God'*
*Written by Stephen Hill*

Published by: Stephen Hill - Ancient Future 2020

Cover design & layout by Tom Carroll

ISBN: 978-0-473-52959-8

This book is also available from Amazon: **www.amazon.com**

More resources can be found at:
**www.ancientfuture.co.nz**

ANCIENT
FUTURE

*Thanks to Tom Carroll, Becky Hill and
Rachel Muir for their invaluable help
in the production of this book.*

# CONTENTS

# CONTENTS

# CHAPTER 1

# DO YOU DESERVE TO BE LOVED BY GOD?

Do you deserve the love of God?

Do you *believe* that you deserve the love of God?

Or do you believe that you *don't* deserve the love of God?

The answer to that question will be crucial in determining how you live your life.

In this book I will answer the question, "Do you deserve the love of God?"

I will answer with an unequivocal 'Yes!'

Human beings deserve the love of God!

It cannot be earned.

It cannot be merited.

But we deserve it.

We have the right to be loved by God.

Our whole purpose is to be loved by God.

What is more, *God* believes that we deserve His love.

I'm not so interested in what I believe in anymore…I'm interested in what God believes.

I want to align myself with God's perspective, with God's hopes, with God's dreams, with what God believes.

Right up front I need to take issue with something. Maybe this is what ultimately motivated me to write what I am writing. Please believe me it is not about the songwriter. I have no doubt that it is an anointed song. It is the song *Reckless Love*. I want to take issue with a single line, the one that goes, "…and I don't deserve it."

I cannot sing that line because it sticks in my craw.

Beloved, we DO deserve the love of God!

We deserve the love of God because God is Love, and we have been created by Love, in Love, through Love, for Love.

That is what I want to address in this book.

I never consider whether my children deserve my love. They never consider whether they deserve my love or not. It doesn't even enter their thoughts. It is a moot point.

It's not just contemporary theology through worship songs that speaks out "I don't deserve it." It's an *age-old* shame-based theology, beginning in the Garden when

Adam and Eve were naked and hid from God because they felt unworthy of His love.

We are so used to living in the Tree of Knowledge and living under condemnation that we assume it is biblical to say that we do not deserve to be loved by God. **That is a massive deception.** The idea of not deserving the love of God is not in Scripture, if we really understand the whole scope of the biblical story. Here is a smattering of verses which declare what the truth really is:

> *But while he was still a long way off, his father saw him and felt compassion, and ran and embraced him and kissed him.* — LUKE 15:20

> *For God so loved the world that He gave His only begotten Son, that whoever believes in Him should not perish but have everlasting life.* — JOHN 3:16

> *In him we live and move and have our being, as even some of your own poets have said, 'For we are indeed his offspring.'* — ACTS 17:28

> *...but God shows his love for us in that while we were still sinners, Christ died for us.* — ROMANS 5:8

> *For I am sure that neither death nor life, nor angels nor rulers, nor things present, nor*

> *things to come, nor powers, nor height nor depth, nor anything else in all creation, will be able to separate us from the love of God in Christ Jesus our Lord.* — ROMANS 8:38,39

> *...in Christ, God was reconciling the world to Himself, not counting their trespasses against them* — 2 CORINTHIANS 5:19

> *But God being rich in mercy, because of the great love with which he loved us, **even when we were dead in our trespasses**.* — EPHESIANS 2:4,5

That last verse pulls the rug out from under the idea that we don't deserve the love of God. God loved us with great love *even when we were dead in our trespasses.*

This issue of "We don't deserve the love of God" is deeply ingrained in our Christianity. Many of us have a theological foundation based on the basic unworthiness of the human creature. God is *saddened* that we view His creation as unworthy. God's creation, though fallen, is inherently good. God *loves* what He has created, especially us, His children.

Many of us cannot adequately receive the Father's love because we still view our humanity through the eyes of the knowledge of good and evil. The blinkers are being removed as divine love seeps ever deeper into our being.

Our 'salvation' is not the beginning. It is a redemption of what was loved first and created. In some ways we need to be more purpose-centred, creation-centred, and less redemption-centred. Original blessing came long before sin. Too many people are unwittingly influenced by the Calvinist (heretical) idea of 'Total Depravity' and, as a result, they cannot receive the substance of God's love. They may be 'saved' but they are not saved into anything of any real joy or power.

I was brought up in a very legalistic denomination. But it wasn't Calvinist. I was brought up on the eternal purpose of God. The hymns that we sang spoke of God's plan before the ages to have sons like Christ before Him in love. That, despite all the legalism, was my theological foundation. My sticking point was that I couldn't receive God's love because of self-judgment. I felt that my human weakness kept me dragging me down from that high calling of sonship. I was deceived in this; weakness is a *crucial feature* of sonship.

I have heard some preachers make the statement; "God doesn't love you because of who you are. He loves you because of who He is." I may have even said that myself. That statement may be useful to a point if you are so love-deficient that you cannot receive His love. The real truth, however, is that God actually does love you because of who you are. His love does not depend on your performance but He is enamoured by you as a parent is enamoured by their child.

Does a mother dote on her child because of who the child is? Of course she does!

Children are conceived in pleasure. Yes, there is brokenness and fallenness but, generally, the very beginning of life, the conception, happens in pleasure. When my wife was pregnant, she had pleasure in what was growing inside her. When our babies were born we looked at them and felt a surge of pleasure and delight. When they grow, they bring so much pleasure. Yes, it can be stressful but we have pleasure in them.

Our pleasure in our children is magnified a millionfold with God. He is delighted and enthralled with His children.

So many of us don't have boldness to come to the Father. We need to get a revelation of our acceptance in sonship before the Father.

Some years ago I dreamt that I was at the entrance gate of a big fairground. It was free entry but a few unscrupulous men were trying to sell tickets at the gate. They were trying to charge people an entrance fee to the fun fair and most people didn't realise that a ticket wasn't needed. In the dream I was challenging the ticket sellers, saying loudly that we didn't need tickets to enjoy the fair.

That is what has happened in our orphan-hearted version of Christianity. We have a right of entry to the Father's presence, but we have been deceived into believing that we need to earn our way into the Father's house. Nothing could be further from the actuality.

Jesus, the Son, came from the Father and this is what it says about Him:

> *But to all who did receive him, who believed in his name, he gave the right to become children of God.* — JOHN 1:12

Knowing this truth in your heart deals with the pseudo ticket sellers. It overrides the legalism that tries to make access into God's presence conditional.

Many Christians think receiving spiritual life is about having to concentrate and try hard. It is actually the opposite. The more relaxed you are the more the Holy Spirit can impart into you because Christianity and the love of God are imparted Spirit to spirit. Be relaxed because the Holy Spirit will still impart into you the spiritual life that is in Him.

# CHAPTER 2

# A DOUBLE
# RECONCILIATION

When I began to receive the love of the Father it wasn't just that I had an experience of lying on the floor laughing or crying.

It was also that I began to believe something different.

My whole foundation of belief began to shift and, actually, that has become much more important than emotional experiences.

I see life with new eyes.

I've seen something and I cannot un-see it and I see it in the Scriptures.

Things have not always been easy. There have been feelings of stress, anger, highs and lows; all of those things.

But the shift in me is this:

I've had a double reconciliation in my heart.

Firstly, at a heart level, I became reconciled to God.

I became reconciled to the One that I had turned away from.

All of my life I was an ardent lover of Jesus but I was full of shame, condemnation and guilt.

Any time I messed up I kept going around in a vicious circle, and I couldn't face God the Father.

Then I became reconciled to a God who loves me unconditionally.

Here's the second thing I became reconciled to. Something equally important.

I became reconciled to myself.

Instead of being under constant guilt,

I was reconciled to God in His true identity while *simultaneously* reconciled to *myself* in my true identity.

It has to be this way.

Because, you see, Christianity is not just about God.

True Christianity is the marriage between God and self.

The marriage of heaven and earth.

It's the marriage of the divine and human.

When the Spirit of God and the spirit within us begin

to synchronise and become as one, we come into peace, we come into rest, we come into fruitfulness, we come into the flow of anointing by the Holy Spirit who lives within us.

I am confident that God wants to take another step with you.

He wants to take a step, further into union with who you are, not only for you to be reconciled with the One who has always loved you.

But, as well as that, for you to be reconciled with *yourself,* so He can come and rest in you and you can begin to accept the presence of God within you.

# CHAPTER 3

# THE RIVER OF PLEASURE

It all begins with the pleasure of God…

He is Love.

He is so happy within Himself.

He has so much pleasure resident within Him and bursting out of Him;

A feeling of happy satisfaction and enjoyment.

Someone wrote a book called "*The Pleasures of Loving God.*"

I've never read it but I think it's a wonderful title

Loving God is meant to be an occupation of deep heartfelt pleasure.

But that is not all…

Long ago, in His eternal heart, God wrote a book called *The Pleasures of Loving Humanity.*

Have you read it?

I want to have pleasure in loving God.

I also want to live in the pleasures of being *loved by* God.

I want to enjoy *receiving* the love of God.

Then I can love Him back.

God is a God who is full of pleasure. God is a God who has pleasure in Himself and is very pleased with life; He has great joy, delight and satisfaction in life.

Out of His pleasure God created.

He fashioned and formed a being,

Called 'Human.'

Male and female in His image.

Then He created a home for love to flourish in:

> *And the Lord God planted a garden in Eden in the East and there He put the man whom He had formed. And out of the garden the Lord God made to spring up every tree that is pleasant to the sight and good for food. The Tree of Life was in the midst of the garden and The Tree of the Knowledge of Good and Evil. A river flowed out of Eden to water the garden and there it divided and became four rivers.* — GENESIS 2:8-10

With the pleasure that flowed out of the heart of God, He planted a garden for us to dwell in, a garden called pleasure, a garden of deep satisfaction of life and well-being.

A river ran out of Eden, out of the sweet garden of pleasure:

> *A river flowed out of Eden to water the garden*
> *and there it divided and became four rivers.*
> — GENESIS 2:10

There is a river of pleasure that flows through creation from the heart of God, from the heart of love.

He is calling us all back into the pleasure of living in the Garden of Eden, back into that personal place in the heart of being delighted in by Him.

God is a God who has so much pleasure within Himself. He is so pleased about who He is and He is so pleased about what He has created and He is so pleased about His children.

The word Eden means 'pleasure.'

That's right — PLEASURE!

In the beginning God planted a garden of pleasure.

A place of pleasure that He delighted in and that He wants His children to delight in.

It says that the river came out of Eden and then it divided into four.

The river came out of *pleasure* and split four ways.

In other words, the river of pleasure flowed out to irrigate the whole earth.

God put humanity in the Garden of Eden to work and to keep it (Genesis 2:15).

The role of the human was to care for the garden of *pleasure*.

God has chosen us, beloved, *you and me*, to be guardians and workers of His *pleasure*.

That is the calling the human person has been given.

Read it this way: "The Lord God took the human and put them in the garden of pleasure to work it and keep it."

You see, God's purpose for us as humans, for those who He delights in, is to be the guardians, the custodians, the developers of His pleasure.

The only criteria given to Adam and Eve was this: They had to avoid eating eat from the Tree of the Knowledge of Good and Evil.

The biggest thing that stops us living in the pleasures of God is the knowledge of good and evil. Trying to determine our own way of pleasing God, trying to assess what's right or wrong, how we can be pleasing to God. Living out of performance and not out of love. When we begin to eat of that, the place of pleasure becomes arid.

Therefore, if the work of the human person is to be 'The Guardian and Custodian of Pleasure, Delight and Wellbeing,' it is of supreme importance to AVOID eating from the Tree of Knowledge.

Because we have eaten of the fruit of the knowledge of good and evil we have been pushed out of the garden of pleasure. But God is bringing us back to the place of His succulent pleasures.

# CHAPTER 4

# A BEAUTIFUL INHERITANCE

I have to say about myself, I am a pleasure lover.

I'm actually a bit of a hedonist.

I find pleasure hard to resist.

I'm drawn towards what I enjoy a lot. It may be different from what other people enjoy but I'm still drawn towards what I enjoy. I find it really difficult to do something that I don't enjoy and often look very grumpy while doing it.

Many years ago I had a job as a manager in a retail store and I couldn't last at it because you have to smile all the time with the customers and if I was going through a bad time I just couldn't keep up a happy face.

I was bought up strictly religious but then my need for pleasure began to rise up because it was always denied and shoved under. I got myself into some trouble. But what I've come to realise, is that while some of the pleasures I sought were false, the *actual motivation* for them wasn't false at all. Why?

It wasn't false because God has *created* me for delight and pleasure.

Pleasure in my relationship with Him.

Pleasure in being me.

Pleasure in my relationship with other people.

Pleasure in my connection with creation.

The more I have begun to align myself with the pleasures of God, with God having pleasure in me and me having delight in myself, temptation to seek false pleasures has begun to fall away.

Do you realise that God has a beautiful inheritance for us to enter into? It is primarily to be found in our connection with Him.

The Psalmist says:

> *The Lord is my chosen portion and my cup;*
> *you hold my lot.*
> *The lines have fallen for me in pleasant places.*
> *Indeed, I have a beautiful inheritance.*
> — PSALM 16:5,6

Beloved, we need to hold onto this reality that the lines for us have fallen in pleasant places. The boundaries of our inheritance are in the place of pleasure.

No matter what's going on in the world, God is essentially a God of pleasure, who has great delight in us and wants us to move into our inheritance in *pleasant* places.

My goal in my speaking and writing is so that we can learn to follow and discover those lines that are in the pleasant places.

I believe with all my heart that the parameters of inheritance are in a pleasant place for all of us.

It is the heart of God.

There is a river of pleasure flowing out of the heart of God to come through us, to connect with us and to flow out of us.

It's not to say we're not going to have heartbreak, difficulty and suffering but I know in my heart that I want to come into that place where there *are pleasures forevermore* and *fulness of joy.* (Psalm 16:11)

David says again in an another Psalm:

> *How precious is your steadfast love, O God!*
> *The children of mankind take refuge in the*
> *shadow of your wings.*
> *They feast on the abundance of your house,*
> *and you give them drink from the river of*
> *your delights.* — PSALM 36:7,8

We can feel the shadow of His wings over us that we can

take refuge in. When we feel safe under the Father's wings we can relax enough to feed on the abundance of His house and begin to drink from the river.

There is a river of love, yes, but there is also a river of *delight* and *pleasure* that flows out of God and I want to drink from it. I don't just want to have a love that comforts me in my brokenness and woundedness, but I also want to go even deeper into the love and discover the river of God's pleasure.

I believe God wants us to keep drinking not only of comfort for our pains and our wounds, but to begin to drink from pleasure. Oftentimes we get focused on healing up our emotions which is needful. In the Father's love there is indeed healing for the soul, but what the Father has called *me* to do is to encourage the *spirit*, to encourage the deepest part of you to drink of the river of pleasure.

You may have had a really messed up life. You may have struggled with injustice, frustration, anger. I know all about it. Maybe your life has gone okay. It is one thing to get that all healed up but I've discovered that if I begin to drink of the river of His pleasure a lot of my struggles can fall away anyway. In my life and in my ministry I am less interested in focusing on what is wrong with people. I want to call forth the new creation. That's what the prophetic does, it speaks to who you really are in God. It calls forth life and potential.

# CHAPTER 5

# GOD IS PLEASED WITH THE HUMAN RACE

God's pleasure came to full fruition when His Son came to earth.

Here is Luke writing about the birth of Jesus:

> *And in the same region there were shepherds out in their field keeping watch, over their flock by night. And an angel of the Lord appeared to them, and the glory of the Lord shone around them, and they were filled with great fear. And the angel said to them, "Fear not, for behold I bring you good news of great joy that will be for all the people. For unto you is born this day in the city of David a Saviour, who is Christ the Lord. And this will be a sign for you, you will find a baby wrapped in swaddling cloths and lying in a manger." And suddenly there was with the angel a multitude of the heavenly host praising God and saying,*

*"Glory to God in the highest and on earth,
peace, good pleasure in men."*

Good pleasure! In what? In humanity!!

The word in the Greek is '*eudokia*' which means 'delight, favour, a feeling of God being proud of humanity'; a feeling of satisfaction, happiness and delight with the human race.

That puts a different spin on it, doesn't it?

Let me set it out for you.

From the time of the Fall right throughout the Old Testament, in the time of the Law, people didn't have a revelation that God was pleased with them. But the angels came to herald the birth of the New Epoch with this statement:

> **"I am pleased with men. I am well satisfied with my creation, the human race. I have pleasure in the humans I have created. And I have so much pleasure in them that I have decided to become one of them myself. Go to Bethlehem and see."**

The whole issue of the New Covenant is that there is no insecurity anymore about whether God is pleased with us or not. The proclamation of the angelic host at the very beginning of the first Christmas is that God has sweet satisfaction in men and women. God is pleased with humans. His heart has pleasure in those He has created and He has sent a Saviour to come and bring us back into that place of pleasure. That's a wonderful thing.

I don't believe those shepherds would have felt condemnation again, because they heard the angelic heavenly host crying out that from now on there is *good pleasure* in humanity. From now on Heaven has declared its enjoyment in the human race.

It seems scandalous, but it is true. It cannot be read any other way.

That's what was heralded at the dawn of the New Covenant of Incarnation, of Sonship to the Father — "*Glory to God in the highest, peace on earth and good pleasure in men.*"

We know that when we look at the earth there's not a lot of peace around. But, you see, *we* are the forerunners to bring peace through us receiving the revelation of God's good pleasure. When God gives you a revelation that He is pleased with the human race, then you can go to the manger in the stable and you can begin to see the movement of God.

The movement of God will, to all intents and purposes, look like a little baby. But you can begin to see how pleased God is to be the Baby. You join the wise men, the shepherds and the holy family at the place where heaven and earth coalesce.

By the way, the wise men were *astrologers*, not astronomers. The wise men were *magi*. It's the same linguistic root as the word 'magic' and the plural of 'magus'.[1] The wise men were the same type of people. Mind-boggling and scandalous, isn't it?

So whether you are a humble (illiterate?) shepherd or you're involved in some dodgy stuff, you have a place at Bethlehem's manger where there is good pleasure in humanity.

At Bethlehem's manger all are equal, and we bow down and worship. When we begin to see His pleasure in us we can begin to see the work of God, the movement of God *even in us.*

At the manger humans came to the incarnated God.

And bowed in wonder.

How did it happen, that He became one of us?

He made the journey from the highest height,

To the stable and the swaddling cloths.

God became a baby.

We need to meet Him there,

In the place of babyhood,

Vulnerability and weakness,

Needing comfort.

---

1. In Acts 8:9-24, some translations refer to Simon the Sorcerer as 'Simon Magus.'

A home for God to relax in.

The work of sonship in you, the work of the Father's love, is making you like Christ, like a baby in a manger, very weak and very vulnerable. That's where the movement of God begins.

As Jesus grew up the pleasure of God continued in and through His Son. When He was baptised something else happened, another development in the ministry of sonship. The heavens were torn open and God the Father expressed pleasure in His Son. The Father said, "This is my beloved Son *in whom I am well pleased*, in whom I have delight and pleasure." That became another foundation in Jesus's life, a foundation to begin to go out and do Kingdom works of power. He was able to confront the activity of Satan when He knew the Father had pleasure in Him.

Jesus then said:

*"Fear not little flock for it is the Father's good pleasure to give you the kingdom."* — LUKE 12:32

Do not doubt or fear.

The Father *wants* to give us the Kingdom.

It is His *pleasure* to give us the Kingdom.

The Kingdom is what the Father gives to us because He loves us.

Do you know what's in the Kingdom?

Freedom.

Freedom from the demonic is in the Kingdom.

Freedom from pain is in the Kingdom.

I'm beginning to hunger again for it, beloved.

To be given the Kingdom, and see the Kingdom work again, coming from the place of sonship.

Jesus told us that it is the Father's delight to give us the Kingdom.

I believe this; if we begin to follow this way of pleasure, we will come into the Kingdom.

When your foundation is right, in sonship, you can follow desire to arrive at the Kingdom,

…because all true pleasure comes out of the place of receiving *His* love and receiving *His* pleasure.

The false pleasures we seek are actually in the wrong Tree.

But the answer to that is not to do away with pleasure.

The answer to that is to get into the *real* pleasure, the *real pleasure* of being loved by Him.

The pleasures of being loved by God and the pleasures of loving God.

That's where life begins to flow, that's where the Kingdom is handed to us.

I'm hoping I will soon have more stories to tell about the coming of the Kingdom. Myself and Becky are hungry for it in the place of sonship. I'm hungrier now, more than ever, for the coming of the Kingdom because it's the Father's good pleasure to give us the Kingdom. It's not enough to just read the words, there's too much crisis out there to just read the words. Humanity has departed from Eden but the answer to all of this is the Kingdom of the Father's pleasure.

# CHAPTER 6

# WHERE THE GODHEAD IS PLEASED TO DWELL

In Colossians 1 verse 19, Paul wrote about Jesus; "For in Him all the fulness of the Godhead was *pleased* to dwell."

When Jesus was on earth He incarnated everything of who God is. That is an incredible statement and we happily accept it, yet we do not really appreciate the dynamic power of it.

Now that is one reality, but wait. There is another:

Paul wrote to the community in Ephesus:

> *And He (God the Father) put all things under His (Jesus') feet and gave Him (Jesus) as head over all things to the Church, which is His (Jesus') body, the fulness of Him (God) who fills all in all.* — EPHESIANS 1:22

This is a further progression in the purposes of God.

The fulness of the Godhead was pleased to dwell in Jesus

but it is *now pleased to dwell in us.*

Can you see it?

The fulness of the Godhead is actually pleased to come and live within us, within the Church.

Are our eyes beginning to open up to it?

Mine are. That's why I love gathering with the spiritual family because the fulness of the Godhead, the river of God's pleasure that was pleased to dwell in Jesus, is actually now pleased to *also* dwell in the *Church.*

We are coming more and more into this reality. Within all of us, as we become family and spiritual community, the fulness of the Godhead is satisfied to dwell. This revelation is gripping me. I'm not in the least interested in promoting myself because I want to be in the Body in which the fulness of the Godhead is living.

Psalm 133 says, *"Behold, how good and pleasant it is for brothers and sisters to dwell together in unity."*

How delightful it is, *how pleasing* to God.

God is extremely pleased with you as an individual but in some senses He is even more pleased when we begin to relate to each other. You can feel it when we are together in unity.

To be honest with you, I've reached a point in my life where I don't feel as much spiritual life as an *individual,* I really don't. Sometimes in my own private life I feel quite dead inside, but I feel it among the Body. I even feel it when I meet up with someone for a coffee. We are not meant to be isolated individuals. The love of the Father is meant to be experienced in the Body.

When I look at my brothers and sisters in Christ I do not see any mess; I really don't!

I see the glory in everyone, not shame and failure.

I see the fulness of the Godhead beginning to emerge among us all. Whether you'll ever be on a stage or not it doesn't really matter.

The Church is coming down off the stage so that we can become the Body!

My desire is not to be some great speaker with thousands of followers on Instagram.

*My* desire is to open our eyes up to see who we really are and to begin to function in the Body of Christ.

# SONSHIP IS THE MEETING PLACE

If God has pleasure in you then His pleasure will also come through you.

God's desire is that His pleasure and your pleasure will become melded together.

He will bring you to a place where you cannot distinguish between what you like and what He likes.

That is the place which sonship occupies.

Sonship occupies a place where everything is reconciled, and where what pleases God and what pleases me comes together.

When I was caught in religion I tried to follow what pleased God but I actually denied my own pleasure. But in sonship there is a synergy of the pleasure of God with my pleasure, becoming one and the same thing.

I don't really ask the question anymore, "God is this your

will or is this just me?" Now I tend to just go with the desire within me because the Spirit indwells me and if it is not in alignment with God He will adjust it. I am beginning to see that His pleasure and my pleasure are becoming one and the same.

God wants to bring us to a place that you enjoy what He enjoys because He enjoys what you enjoy.

There is a great purpose in beginning to realise that God also enjoys what we enjoy. It's not to let us off the hook so that we can just do what we like for selfish purposes.

For God is still calling us to be like His Son.

Sonship is the place where it all comes together.

There needs to be a synchronicity of God with our human selves.

Because we cannot experience the love of God outside of our human existence.

God, our Father, Jesus, the Holy Spirit, is a God who is full of joy. The Trinity is a trinity of deep joy and deep pleasure.

God's love is not a grumpy love or a holding back love.

It's an exuberant love gushing from a pleasure-loving God.

God is a God with a river of pleasure flowing out of Him.

His basic foundational reality is love and it's a love of great elation and enjoyment, of great satisfaction, of great pleasure in those who He created.

Out of the pleasure of His love He created us to be loved by Him. When you were conceived in the Father's heart it was out of the pleasure of God, no matter what way you were conceived. Whether you're legitimate or illegitimate, or whatever, the Father's pleasure is still there. When you were born the river of pleasure still flowed through. And the river of pleasure has been flowing unabated. That river flowed from eternity and it flowed through creation. Satan attempted to stymie it but it has flowed on and on, through the patriarchs, prophets, kings and psalmists. It flowed through creation and through redemption. The river of pleasure keeps flowing.

In Revelation 22 the angel shows John that this river of the water of life, the river of His pleasure, is still flowing. Everything is coming to a conclusion in the river of the water of life flowing from the throne of God and the Lamb.

Reconnect with the river of God's pleasure. Right here, right now. His pleasure is dripping over us, it is coursing through our veins.

The angels spoke the truth; *Glory to God in the highest, on earth peace and good pleasure in all humanity.*

Holy Spirit wants to show you who you are in God

and call you back into the garden again, the garden of the Father's pleasure.

The Father dreamt you up, He conceived you and He brought you forth.

He is totally confident in His ability to see His desires met. He is confident in the victory that Jesus has accomplished on the Cross.

Now take time to reconnect with the river of pleasure that flows through the heart of the Father,

Receive what He's saying over you.

Hear His voice being uttered over you, "*The one in whom I am well pleased, in whom is My delight…*"

# CHAPTER 8

# WHAT IS SPECIAL ABOUT HUMANS?

For most of my life I didn't take much notice of Creation or the spirituality of Creation. That is changing. I am seeing that Creation is an amazing place in which the Spirit of God dwells. The Spirit of God is pulsating in Creation.

This may boggle your mind but your heart gets it. Your spirit is already understanding it and will understand in ever increasing measure.

It's one thing for us to believe but it's a very different thing for us to agree, understand and be aligned with what *God* believes.

Like I said…

I'm not so interested in what I believe anymore,

I'm more interested in what God believes.

What does God believe about you and me, about the human race?

I want to take you further on this journey as you read this book.

What is it about humans? What is so special about us, the human race?

I want to turn to Psalm 8.

The Psalmist talks to the LORD,

He wonders in amazement how great God is:

> *Oh Lord, our Lord, how majestic is your*
> *name in all the earth!*
> *You have set your glory above the heavens.*
> *Out of the mouths of babies and infants,*
> *you have established strength because of*
> *your foes,*
> *to still the enemy and the avenger.*
> — PSALM 8:1,2

David understands something very important as he contemplates the majesty of creation.

Here it is:

As we become childlike, the voice of the enemy will be silenced.

If you become like a baby the voice of the accuser will begin to quieten down and be stilled.

It's absolutely true!

Back to Psalm 8: David ponders in amazement,

> *When I look at the heavens, the work of*
> *your fingers,*
> *the moon and the stars that you have set*
> *in place.*
> — PSALM 8:3

Then he turns to himself, the weak, vulnerable human being, and wonders:

> *What is man that you are mindful of him,*
> *and the son of man that you care for him?*
> — PSALM 8:4

Why, great God, are you so interested in humans?

We are in the midst of this incredible creation and we look at our little selves and we seem so insignificant but the Psalmist has this insight:

> *Yet you have made him a little lower than*
> *the heavenly beings and crowned him with*
> *glory and honour.*
> — PSALM 8:5

You may be a little lower than the heavenly beings but *you are crowned with glory and honour.*

You may look at yourself and think you've got problems but Father believes you are crowned with glory and honour. That is His purpose for you. That is how He sees you. Not as an afterthought but as a *forethought.*

> *You have made him a little lower than the*
> *heavenly beings…and you have given him*
> *dominion over the works of your hands.*
> — PSALM 8:5,6

Are you struggling with that? Can you embrace the truth of that statement? You have *dominion* over the works of His hands.

That is the way He sees you. This is me speaking from Father into the core of your identity. You, beloved ones, have a New Creation Identity that is more fundamental than anything that you have ever struggled with.

Some of us have had privileged lives, some of us have had lives that are full of trouble, some of us have a lot of stuff to work through, but you also have a New Creation Identity that is not dependent on a lot of that stuff.

The purpose of us becoming healed and delivered is so that our minds and emotions would be liberated to live aligned with how our Father sees us and be increasingly free to express ourselves.

You may look at yourself and think you are not a very whole person. You want to be healed and whole — and that's a good thing.

But when you *are* healed and whole, what do you think

you are going to look like? Are you going to look like Stephen Hill? Are you going to look like someone else?

The truth is, you haven't a clue what you are going to be like. You may have an ideal: *If I was more whole I could do this or that*, but you have absolutely no concept what God has intended for you. It is beyond your comprehension because Father is bringing us into wholeness not merely to live a nice life and have no problems.

Father is bringing us into wholeness for a much greater purpose. He wants to express the image of His Son in and through us. There is part of us that is already whole and has never ever been affected by anything negative. That is the deepest part of who we are, our true identity in the Spirit.

As the Psalmist says:

> *You have given him dominion over the*
> *works of your hands,*
> *and you have put all things under his feet,*
> *all sheep and oxen, and also the beasts of the*
> *fields,*
> *the birds of the heavens, and the fish of the*
> *sea and whatever passes along the paths of*
> *the seas.*
> *O Lord our Lord, how majestic is your name*
> *in all the earth.*
> — PSALM 8:6-9

Long before Christ arrived on earth, David understood that God acknowledged humanity's place within the creation, to be God's representatives. That status as the Guardian of Creation was mandated at the very outset of human existence on this earth:

> *God created humanity in His own image*
> *In the image of God he created him.*
> *Male and female He created them.*
> — GENESIS 1:27

Male and female are created in the image of God because God is both masculine and feminine. We are in the image of God in order to have dominion. Dominion must come out of harmony.

What has happened in the earth since The Fall is that dominion has been lost. It has been lost partly because of Satan's war against the feminine aspect of God's image. Dominion has become domination. Humans have lost the ability to nurture and protect Creation and, as a result, Creation is suffering. Only the restoration of the delicate balance of the masculine and feminine image *together* can have dominion and bring healing and new life to Creation.

The only thing that can really rule is the image of God. In authority, yes, but also in nurturing and comfort. The Kingdom of God is a Kingdom of the expression of God's love.

CHAPTER 9

# A STEP FURTHER

In Hebrews, the writer quotes from Psalm 8 but takes it a step further.

If we turn to Hebrews 2, the writer quotes directly from Psalm 8:

> *What is man, that You are mindful of him,*
> *Or the son of man that You care for him.*
> *You made him for a little while lower than*
> *the angels;*
> *You have crowned him with glory*
> *and honour,*
> *Putting everything in subjection under*
> *his feet.*
> — HEBREWS 2:6-8

The writer to the Hebrews quotes this to distinguish between angels and humans. Now let me tease this out because it may surprise you.

The point the Hebrews author makes here is that God actually values humans as *superior* to the angelic beings.

Did you notice a subtle difference between Psalm 8 and the Hebrews author quoting it?

In verse 7 in Hebrews the words "*for a little while*" are added, which are not in Psalm 8.

Our place beneath the angels *is only temporary* because our destiny is to rule the world to come!

Look at Hebrews 2, verse 5:

*.... for it was not to angels that God subjected the world to come.*

Tell me, do you still believe that you don't deserve the love of God?

The human person, that is *you* and *I*, is the very *highest point* of God's purposes, the *apex* of God's creation.

We have been conceived of, designed, and formed to rule the coming world in a new creation of love and sinlessness for ever. We are called to partner with God in reversing the effects of The Cosmic Disaster that began when Lucifer fell.

So you are not just here on earth to muddle through, or even to get healed up and live a better life.

That is a laudable enough goal in itself but there is a much greater purpose than that.

You are not here just because God has reluctantly decided to pour a little bit of love out on you.

You have been created by Love, out of Love, in Love, through Love, for Love, to be loved eternally by your Heavenly Father.

We are the very highest product of His divine genius.

Us little humans are the jewel of His crown.

So much so that He actually became one of us, through His Son Jesus.

Not as an afterthought or a blip.

But as His objective from a past eternity.

Jesus is still human. How amazing. Heaven contains a human, at the Father's right hand.

What is more, He remains human for ever.

God has committed Himself completely to the human person.

He has not merely invested in us.

There is no going back, as far as God is concerned.

He made a total commitment to the human race for ever.

His Son is eternally one of us!

The Father is not reluctant to love you. The Father sees us in a way that will take us eternity to realise.

Father sees us having everything under subjection, under

our feet. It's written right here in Hebrews:

> *Now in putting everything in subjection to him, he has left nothing outside of his control*
> — HEBREWS 2:8

Who is he talking about here?

**This is *not* talking about *Jesus*. This is talking about *humans*; little old me and little old you.**

God is saying...*I am putting* **everything** *in subjection to man.*

I, God, have left nothing outside of humanity's control.

Hebrews 2:8 goes on:

> *At present we do not yet see everything in subjection to him.*

This, again, is talking about ourselves, human people.

Yes, God has put everything potentially under our dominion.

However, at present we do not see that.

At present the best we can do to walk on water is a stand-up paddle board.

At present everything is not in subjection to us.

We do not have the faith to absolutely heal all sickness

and dispel death.

Then it says....

> *But we see him who for a little while was*
> *made a little lower than the angels, namely*
> *Jesus, crowned with glory and honour...*
> — HEBREWS 2:9.

Jesus is the prototype. He went before us.

He too was made lower than the angels, but *for a little while.*

Now He is crowned with glory and honour.

*And we are going where Jesus is.*

Jesus is the archetype, the forerunner of sonship.

We don't see everything subjected to ourselves *but we are going to see it happen.* Why?

Because Jesus is now crowned with glory and honour and the Father's purpose for you and for me is to crown *us* with glory and honour, sharing the Father's throne with the Firstborn Son.

# THE FAMILY CULTURE

When we are bought up as children we grow up in a family culture. There is nothing you can do about that. Positive or negative, it is what it is.

I was bought up in my family culture but I'm talking about *THE* family culture. There is a family culture of the Heavenly Father who sees everything as subject to us. It even says in Hebrews 1:14 that we humans are not God's servants, the *angels* are the servants. The angels are ministering spirits sent out to serve for the sake of those who are to inherit salvation.

The angels are there to do work for us.

We are the family, they are the employees.

We can have the angels to help us because we are the absolute crown of God's creation.

I believe Father wants us to really begin to walk into his supernatural resources. That can feel overwhelming but one of the reasons we cannot step into that is because of things like condemnation. We cannot step into that because we feel unworthy. We don't see ourselves as the princes and princesses of the royal family.

But we are in Christ and we have the same authority as He does.

I want to communicate the Heavenly family culture to you.

I want to speak the Father's DNA into you.

I want to speak new creation identity into you.

Sometimes we try to get our old orphan identities healed.

In reality, however, that is not our real identity.

Our real identity is in Christ

We are from the same Source and one with Him.

This is new creation but it is also more ancient than anything that has gone before. The New Covenant is way before the Old Covenant.

Christianity is more ancient than Judaism.

Christianity is the life that God Himself lives.

The Trinity live in New Covenant reality and have always done so. The story of redemption is to bring mankind into the original purpose of God, and in the New Testament we see it unveiled.

We are shown the true reality of what is going on, what God has always been unfolding. So whatever is 'new' is actually very, very ancient.

The future that we are going into is connecting us with things that are thousands, millions, billions of years old.

It is from eternity past to eternity future.

Loved by endless Love.

# CHAPTER 11

# GLORIFIED BY GOD

Just before He went to the cross, Jesus talked with His Father. John puts it like this:

> *When Jesus had spoken these words, He lifted*
> *up His eyes to heaven and said,*
> *"Father the hour has come;*
> *Glorify your Son that the Son may glorify*
> *You..." —* JOHN 17:1

As I grew up I was deceived by religion. The deception was that I had to glorify God first before He would glorify me. I believed I had to live a life pleasing to Him so that, in return, I would receive blessing and anointing. But what Jesus says here is that the Father has to glorify the Son *first.*

That's different. That's not how I thought it works.

Why does God glorify the Son before the Son glorifies God?

The Father had to reveal who Jesus was as His Son so that the Son could really show who He, the Father, is.

This does not only apply to Jesus.

*You* cannot glorify the Father without the Father glorifying *you* first.

The problem with religion is that everybody is trying to glorify God in order to receive something from God.

It is actually the other way around.

The Father is glorifying you first.

He is making you shine in who you really are; that's what glory is, you shining out of your personality.

The Father is making your personality shine out first so that you will become a glorification of who He is and when people see you, the Father will be glorified.

The initiative has come from Him first. Jesus said to Him, *"You've got to glorify the Son so that the Son can glorify You."*

This turns it around.

You cannot give glory to the Father unless you've been glorified first.

Believe me, you can't.

If you try and do that, you'll be led to the Tree of the Knowledge of Good and Evil and that is a path that leads to death.

If you're not glorified in your personality you can't

manifest the unique part of the Father's personality that He wants to show through you.

We all are meant to display something of the Father's personality. The preacher up the front doesn't have any more of the Father's personality than you do. You display a part of the Father's personality that they could never show. The Father is glorifying sons and daughters to then shine forth who He is because we're the reflection of His personality here on earth and in all creation.

In the old Westminster Catechism it says that, *"Man's chief end is to glorify God and enjoy Him forever."*

I want to say it in a different way.

**Man's chief end is to be *glorified* by God and to then glorify God and enjoy and manifest Him forever.**

Our forefathers who wrote out the Westminster Catechism sort of missed what Jesus said in John 17.

Or maybe they assumed it only applied to Him.

I believe it applies to *all* sons and daughters.

The chief end of humanity is first to be glorified by God and then to glorify Him because when you are glorified by Him it is Father telling you who you are, Spirit to spirit.

We need to receive affirmation from Father first and then our lives will bring Him glory.

Father wants to declare who He sees you as.

So you can give up on the struggle.

Take some time off from striving to receive Father's love and go out and enjoy yourself and as you do that you will begin seeing Father take initiatives towards you.

I want to take the pressure off you a little because you are here to be glorified by God.

Take a step back into rest and watch it happen.

CHAPTER 12

# EVERYONE HAS A PART TO PLAY

Albert Einstein said this:

> *"Everybody is a genius. But if you judge a fish by its ability to climb a tree, it will live its whole life believing that it is stupid."*

That statement is about human potential. Einstein's point was that the education system is designed for everyone to be academic and pass exams and get assessed on the same criteria. Many of us thought we were stupid because the rigid education system didn't fit who we really are. It's the same in the workplace.

Climbing the tree is either about success or failure.

A fish will inevitably fail to climb the tree, even though it can expertly swim in water.

It was never designed to climb the tree.

The Christian Church has fallen into the same trap.

Here's my adaptation of Einstein's quote:

> *Everyone is anointed. But if you judge a person by their ability to preach or lead worship, then they will live their whole life thinking they have no anointing.*

The way we run our church meetings is like the tree. It's pretty much limited to the specific programme organised by the local church. On Sunday, if you are not up front on the stage you are passive; there is nothing for you to do but be the audience. As a result, a division has appeared. Those on the stage are 'in ministry' and the rest of us are not 'in ministry.'

We are not all monkeys. We cannot all climb the tree.

But some of us are fish.

This is where God is taking us.

The whole way of being the Body of Christ, the Church, will shift and change more and more as we come into sonship. Sons and daughters are not going to just sit and warm seats. Sons and daughters won't be satisfied to be an audience or 'the congregation.' Sons and daughters are not sermon fodder.

The purpose of true ministry, according to Ephesians 4:12, is for the equipping of the saints, because we are God's representatives to Creation.

Authentic ministry must elevate the Body and give the saints what they need to become who God sees them to be.

We don't go to church, we *are* the Church.

The true purpose of the five-fold ministry in Ephesians is to work themselves out of a job.

Ministry is a temporary thing until *we all* arrive at the stature and fulness of Christ, until we all come to maturity. (Ephesians 4:13)

Anyone who sees themselves as an apostle or prophet (or whatever) and doesn't see that they're supposed to be working themselves out of a job by promoting the saints and lifting them up, is not doing apostolic work, or prophetic work or true ministry.

I read recently that one of the definitions for 'apostle' in the Greek is 'under-rower.'

In other words, the slaves in the bottom of the ship (in Greek or Roman times) who did the rowing down underneath the deck. These galley-slaves were the lowest of the low, whipped by overseers to keep the ship moving forward. That's the apostles, hidden below deck.

The true function of apostolic and prophetic ministry is to be hidden underneath, in the foundations, to lift *you* up so that *you* are glorified and celebrated. Our contemporary Christian culture has got it the wrong way around. Apostle this, prophet so and so — big ministries — it's not the genuine article. The true function of the five-fold ministry is to *release you* into *your* ministry, toward others and ultimately towards Creation.

Creation is waiting for the sons of God to appear but it's not going to happen only through seminars and conferences. That's a tiny part of the big picture. Creation is waiting for us to appear through *life*.

There is no sacred/secular division. You too can flow in your anointing. even if you're never called to be a speaker. We can get frustrated that we are missing God's plan for our lives. That feeling of missing God's plan may only be there because a sacred/secular split is operative within us and we cannot really see where God is calling us. We think the only way into God's calling is through Bible College.

The Kingdom of God is so much bigger than we ever thought it was. My wife, Becky, is extremely talented and intelligent and she is very good at relating to people; she is great at just going and speaking to people cold, just chatting to them. I'm not very good at small talk but she is. Becky just gets chatting to people at the school gate or in the grocery store. She once became close friends with a lady who was a refugee from Iraq, a Muslim who wore the hijab.

Now that could never have happened for me; I've watched too many documentaries. Becky's got a very simple, winsome way of meeting people exactly where they're at.

I've read too many history books, that just wouldn't work for me.

But the pressure is off me. The mission of reaching the world is not down to me as an individual. It's for the *entire* Body of Christ.

You can only ever be yourself.

We are all *so varied*. Real ministry is the expression of who God is through you. This is what we are beginning to come into.

Take two of the main foundational apostles of the *Ekklesia* (the Church),

Peter and Paul.

Personally, I identify more with Paul. I was bought up religious, a bit of an intellectual, bigoted and zealous.

Peter was pretty much the exact opposite. He was a man's man, wasn't sophisticated and intellectual, wore his heart on his sleeve, a verbal processor.

Yet Peter, big bluff Peter, became a major foundation post of the Church.

He wasn't a bookish man, like Paul. Mind you, Paul was no wimp.

If you're like Peter and don't feel like reading, that's fine, because Peter, the fisherman, was not brought up in the rabbinical school like Paul. If you read the gospels Peter was one step forwards, two steps backwards, big time.

But Peter, says:

> *But you are a chosen race, a royal priesthood, a holy nation, a people for His own possession that you may proclaim the excellencies of Him who called you out of darkness into His marvellous light. Once you were not a people but now you are God's people. Once you had not received mercy but now you have received mercy.* — 1 PETER 2: 9,10

God is speaking into our identity as a royal priesthood and a holy nation, a people that He desires to possess, to live in as His inheritance.

Later, in 2 Peter 1:3, it says,

> *His divine power has granted to us all things that pertain to life and godliness, through the knowledge of Him.*

You see, you can only become godly through the knowledge of Him. Whatever being 'godly' means.

I think it means *being full of God.*

I used to believe that a godly person never had fun!

All of you are godly. Can you believe that?

Can you believe that you are a godly person as you are, without any more change? Can you believe that?

If you even *begin* to believe that in your heart, you will start to see the things that are granted to you for life. Peter goes on:

> *...Him who has called us to His own glory and excellence, by which He has granted to us His very great and precious promises so that through them you may become partakers of the divine nature...* — 2 PETER 1:3,4

Now, I admit, a lot of times you and I don't feel like a partaker of the divine nature but that is what it says *we are*.

As we receive love we are drinking the divine nature. If you can open your heart a tiny bit, that is actually enough. You don't even have to open your whole heart the whole way because if you can open your heart just a little crack, what's going to come into it is the divine nature — LOVE — and divine love will give you confidence to open up a little bit more, a little bit more, a little bit more.

Father is here to give you confidence to open even a little crack and I believe with all of my heart that every single person has partaken of the divine nature and that will continue to flow through you.

You don't have to be like other people. You only have to be yourself. You can be a very simple person and just be yourself and go out there and have fun. You don't have to read a book! You can be like Peter if you want.

Paul never walked on water, but Peter did.

If you're not a studious person don't try and strive to be one. If you're not an academic I release you from the tyranny of study.

Be like Peter!

You may think you are not as smart or as spiritual as someone else.

But...you are still a partaker of the divine nature.

# CHAPTER 13

# THE GLORY OF SONSHIP

God has created us humans for a very special purpose: To be His children and live in His inheritance.

Have you ever considered *this*?

If Christ is the mediator between God and man (1 Timothy 2:5), which He is, as the Son…

**Then sons and daughters are the mediators between Christ and creation.**

This is the glory of sonship.

A son (male or female) is a person who carries within themselves, in their humanness, the divine nature.

That is what God wants on this earth; sons and daughters like His first-born.

He wants us to be the meeting place between heaven and earth so that heaven and the anointing and the Spirit and the divine is mediated *through us* to those around us and to creation.

Your heart already knows this and your heart wants it. Your heart and spirit want to connect with creation. It's so natural to us. God is not wanting to take us away from this; God is wanting to meld heaven and earth *together*.

One of the things that the prophetic movement needs to be careful of is getting disconnected from the natural; becoming too mystical, too ethereal. They think it is being focused on heaven but it is somewhat misplaced.

True Christianity is the joining of heaven and earth.

Real Christianity brings heaven into the solid and the tangible.

It is down in the dirt and the mess.

True Christianity is the synthesis of spirit, soul, mind *and body*. Eternally we're going to have *bodies*.

A lot of the teaching about heaven is too mystical and ethereal. In heaven, whatever that means, we are not going to be floating around like ghosts.

We are going to have *bodies*, glorified *bodies*.

There is going to be a new heaven and a new *earth*.

A renewed earth is an integral part of God's future purpose.

On the other hand, some people think (secretly); *heaven*, how boring! All we will be doing will be sitting on clouds playing harps for eternity. I'm the only person I know who actually does want to play a harp in heaven. I love the music of the Celtic harp, the national instrument of Ireland!

Heaven, whatever that means (we don't really know), is way beyond our wildest dreams. Everything we love and enjoy about life here on earth is a shadow of what heaven is going to be like. If you think it is wonderful here, and heaven is going to be like a long, boring Sunday service, believe you me it won't be.

The reality of heaven may well involve us living on a renewed earth. It could likely mean bringing greenness and teeming life to planets throughout the cosmos. I don't know. There is much speculation but whatever it is, heavenly reality is actually solid too. It's based in your body. We will have *glorified bodies*.

The spirit of sonship is not just a heavenly thing.

It is heavenly *and* earthly.

It's all connected.

A son and a daughter is the meeting place of not only heaven but also earth.

Don't worry if you hardly have the concentration to read a book.

If you'd rather have your head in an engine, don't be afraid to dive into that engine.

If you'd rather have your hands in the soil or work with the kids, go for it!

Forget about the books! Go with who you are and you will find that you are the meeting place of heaven and earth as you turn the spanner, as you cook or…you fill in the blank.

Now, in some ways I'm not much earthly good. I'm not down on myself; I just know that I've been painted into a corner by God and by myself because all I can do is some speaking and writing. Most of the jobs I ever did were below my level of intelligence. If I had gone down a different track when I was younger I may have become a journalist or a lecturer or something, but I'm beyond that now. In saying that, I am more and more earthed. If a Christian is trying to escape from the earth it's not going to happen because Heaven is *coming down*. Heaven is coming down to dwell within your mess, your dirt, and your very base humanness.

A true son (male and female) is someone in whom heaven and earth converge.

They're a heavenly person, not because they're super-spiritual but because they know their true identity. They're also earthly because they are able to be on the earth and connect to others, connect to real life, connect to creation and bring heavenly reality in. God is creating us to be fully human but also 'divine' in the sense that we carry the Holy Spirit. That is sonship.

# CHAPTER 14

# PARTNERS WITH GOD

God has created us to be partners with Him in the work He is doing. God created the human person to co-participate with the Divine. We are to be the co-worker, the business partner, of the Divine.

Again I say it with the greatest respect and love – this whole thing about 'I don't deserve it' — it's a nice line and we sing it without giving it much thought — but it ain't true! It comes from a shame-based theology. The thing is you *do* deserve it because you are created for it, from the foundations of the world to be a co-partner with the Divine as His adored sons and daughters.

Adam and Eve were actually created to be God's co-workers in creation. Adam and Eve were created to augment God's creation work.

When God formed creation the only thing that was cultivated was the Garden of Eden itself.

Some people think that what is recorded in the first chapter of Genesis was not the original creation. In their understanding, the Genesis account largely described the *re-creation* of the original. This theory is based in Isaiah 45:18 where some translations say that God did not create the earth waste and empty whereas if you read in Genesis it says the earth *was* waste and empty.

Satan had already fallen when man and woman were put in Eden. If that is true, the purpose of man and woman was to cultivate and help God restore what had already fallen through the Fall of Satan.

The other perspective is that the account in Genesis 1 is about the original creation. If *that* is true, then God created a creation which needed completing. Work needed to be done to extend the Garden of Eden throughout the earth.

In some ways, it doesn't matter which of these is true.

Here is the point I driving at.

What I'm saying is that the man and the woman, Adam and Eve, were put on earth to be *partners* with God in His work of creation and building, developing and restoring the creation. Whatever way you look at it, we are not here as robots or pawns. We are the very crown of God's creation.

We deserve to be loved by God!

Your purpose is not to get it all together so you struggle a little bit less. Your calling is more than just getting your stuff sorted.

God sees you in a much more powerful way than how you see yourself. This is even meant to redeem the ordinary because your calling may actually be to sweep the streets, work in a grocery store or be a caregiver. There is nothing inferior if that is how God expresses Himself.

There is no division between being in ministry and not being in ministry. Whenever sonship begins to flow through you, you will *automatically* find yourself in ministry.

We are *all* in ministry because ministry is the overflow of Christ within, in whatever situation we're in, whatever your gifting or calling is.

Calling and gifting is not something brought to us in salvation.

It is given to us at creation, when we are little children.

I used to think that Paul was something special when he said that he was called from his mother's womb (Galatians 1:15), but it's actually true for all of us.

We have *all* been called from our mother's womb because God has put creation gifts within us, hardwired into our humanity.

God has called us to be with Him in the garden again. The garden is the place where the human and the divine work together, where God gives us something and says, "Here you go, you do what you feel with it." So you start to tend it and work it. A garden is not something that is just completely left to nature. I'm fully aware that many farming methods are destroying the earth but the true garden and true dominion is where man and God are partnering together to bring restoration. Spiritual ministry, like gardening, is the partnership of you with your Father. God is bringing us in to partner with Him, to create Eden. Creation groans for the restoration of Eden-life.

Remember what I wrote earlier; the word Eden means 'pleasure.' I'm sure religious people don't like that!

Father is going to give a new permission to follow pleasure, to be guided, not necessarily by servile command, but to be led by pleasure, like a child.

Some of your future direction in hearing from God can be through pleasure or through compassion rather than, "Oh, I must hear from God whether He will want me to do this or that."

You can begin to hear God through your emotions, even through your body. We are to be incarnated carriers of the divine so you can even be led to a place through pleasure and if it's not healthy for you Father will sort that out. Don't worry about it. My children are very motivated by pleasure; they go at it like bees to a honey pot. It's not their responsibility to make judgments about what's healthy for them and what's not healthy for them. Not yet anyway. It is the parents' responsibility.

Babies do not take responsibility for what's right and what's wrong. They just grab what is put in front of them, whether it's good for them or not. They don't intervene for themselves, the *parent* intervenes. The Father is a perfect parent. If you want to know what it is to be parented by God, be open to getting things wrong because God will then begin to parent you.

We don't experience God's individual parenting of us precisely because we are not willing to make mistakes. When you are willing to mess up and go out and dive into the mud and eat the chocolate cake, you will discover the very nuanced parental care of the heavenly Parent! You will find that Father will regularly tend to you. He might say, "No son, that's not good for you, it's bad for baby's teeth!" He might say, "Come to Daddy, darling, get your nappy changed."

I am talking about spiritual experience here. You may be a mature person, have big responsibilities in life, but this can still be how your heart relates to God. Our hearts are not designed to be anything other than childlike. You could be a CEO of a business but need Daddy to put you down for a nap. Seriously. I'm fifty-five years old but I have now learned to live in my heart like a little child (while at the same time being a husband and a father) and Father parents me. My relationship to my wife and kids is not childish but it does flow from my childlike connection to my Papa.

Okay, so what does all this mean?

It means you can doubt yourself less.

You can believe in yourself.

You can become more aware of the life of the Spirit.

You can trust the process of His work in you.

You can believe in God within you.

# CHAPTER 15

# HOW TO RECEIVE GUIDANCE AS A SON OR DAUGHTER

Are you trying to hear God more accurately?

Are you interested in learning to discern the voice of God, to hear Him better, to understand more about what He wants for your life?

I have a surprise for you.

It is different when you come into sonship.

Most of us have been to seminars or read books about how to hear from God. I have done my fair share of this myself.

It was good. I benefited from it at the time, but I see something now that I didn't see then.

A lot of what I was taught was actually an orphan-hearted (slave mentality) way of hearing from God.

Here is the general gist of this 'technique' of discerning

the voice of God. First of all, we are listening for a command for something to go and do.

Then, it's a process of elimination. A thought enters your mind and the big question is, "Is this the Devil, is it me, or is it God?"

You have to start dismissing every alternative until you're convinced that your random thought is God talking to you. After getting rid of the possibility of it being Satan, and then pouring cold water on your own desires (which *cannot possibly* be the same as God's will!) what you are left with is the voice of God. I am being a bit dramatic but does this sound familiar?

This method of hearing from God is not reliable. Here's why:

For a start, the voice of Satan is not so clearly discerned as you may think.

Satan will not always whisper temptation to do naughty things in your ear.

Satan is very religious.

Satan will also entice you into feeling condemned.

Satan will make you feel bad about yourself.

One of Satan's priorities is to make you feel unworthy.

He is very happy for you to believe that you don't deserve

the love of God.

That belief will keep you trapped in shame.

Satan will push you into self-energised religion, into a karma-wheel of condemnation and striving.

The good news is, however, it's not meant to be that way. What a relief!

You can start receiving guidance and hearing from God in a much wider way than you ever thought possible.

Let me tell you, in sonship you can hear from God because the more we grow in His love, the voice of God and our voice become *reconciled*.

The more you harmonise with the Father the less distinction there will be between your inner dialogue and His whisperings to you.

The true form of guidance in Christianity and in sonship is **incarnational guidance.**

In other words, the God who lives within you melds His thinking and synchronises His voice with your own thoughts, feelings and desires.

You can begin to go on a journey of experimenting and trusting that, and see what happens.

Permission is granted to start to enter into *incarnational guidance* rather than just trying to hear the voice of God.

Incarnational guidance means that the will of God is already resident and operative through your own self.

When you are rooted and grounded in the love of the Father, you can hear the voice of God through your own emotions, through your desire, through your pleasure, through your repulsion.

The more we come into alignment with Him incarnationally the closer we will be to His will for our lives.

The guidance of sons and daughters is not like going into work every morning where your line manager tells you to do such and such.

It's more like your Dad is the owner of the business and increasingly brings you into His vision for what He wants to accomplish and gives you the go-ahead to try stuff out.

In sonship permission is *already* granted because sonship is Trinity-Spirit wrapped in flesh. That is the goal of sonship.

The very life of God Himself is interwoven, mixed, stirred into our humanness.

I am only beginning to take little steps in this myself. This is the way to discern God's voice.

He is not an external boss or commander. He is a Father, and a Son, who lives internally by the Spirit in you and I.

When your spirit and soul (mind, will and emotions)

become aligned with the love of God, then you can use your mind, will and emotions as guidance. Try not to second-guess your motivations, thoughts and desires but run with them and if the peace of God stays with you then you are progressing down the pathways of His will.

Rather than trying to hear from God up front, a more authentic way in sonship is to follow our inclinations and then use the presence or absence of the peace of God as the indicator of whether to push further or change direction. The way of freedom is that we have the peace of God resident within us, and we live our life according to the impulses of our heart, but if we make a decision or take a direction which causes that peace to be disturbed, then that is how we know we have gone on a tangent from what the Spirit is doing.

I heard Bill Johnson say something like, "Many Christians try to crucify the resurrected life." I wholeheartedly agree with that very astute observation. He meant, I believe, that many believers are so sceptical about the work of God in their hearts that they inadvertently stymie it.

Let me put it like this: If you have wholeheartedly surrendered your life to God, you can be sure that He has heard you and that He believes your sincerity. From that basis, pretty much everything has already been crucified, and you can begin to trust that what you are now living in is resurrection life, and you can begin to follow it.

I admit this seems quite simplistic, but I truly believe it is as uncomplicated as that. Much of the process we go through is God outworking this truth in our experience.

Here's another thought:

Sonship runs through your body.

Sonship runs through the very muscles and cells of your body.

You can be guided by the energy of your body, it's incarnational.

Don't try and work it out. Just feel it and begin to move in it.

I'm just hoping sonship runs through my body enough to lose about twenty kilograms!! Believe me, that has worked for me before.

I've started to try and listen to my body a lot more.

Paul knew this. He writes:

> *...do you not know that your body is a temple of the Holy Spirit within you. You are not your own, for you were bought with a price. Now glorify God in your body.*
> — 1 CORINTHIANS 6:19,20

Yes, Paul wrote this when he was dealing with sin issues, but the point he was making was this: when we divorce our body from the indwelling Spirit we will go astray. The only way to resist temptation is to love the temple, to love and honour our bodies as the house of God.

How about reconciling yourself with the temple of the Holy Spirit?

I mean *your body*.

You don't glorify God in your body by sublimating it through your willpower. You allow the Resident within to make Himself known and you feel Him in and through your body.

What does it mean to glorify God in your body? It doesn't necessarily mean being a martyr. Neither does it mean going down to the gym and pumping up the muscles. However, I won't dismiss either of these; it is up to God. We may be called upon to give our physical lives, who knows? It is also important not to neglect our physical health. Spirit, soul and body are all inextricably inter-connected.

The resurrected life runs through our bodies; it is incarnational. When Jesus was resurrected He said to His disciples, "I'm hungry, give me something to eat." He sat on the beach and cooked fish over the fire, in *resurrection life*. Resurrection life is not some floaty thing. It's incarnated, manifested now, and ultimately, in a bodily form.

# CHAPTER 16

# FREEDOM TO EXPLORE

When you get free of condemnation you will discover something that takes a bit of getting used to.

You are the will of God.

No, I didn't make a mistake here. It wasn't a typo. YOU are the will of God!

As a son and as a daughter you are the will of God increasingly.

In our orphan experience we were on a futile quest to reach a state of being in the 'perfect will' of God (Romans 12:2).

Now, instead of being paralysed trying to discover the perfect will of God, you are increasingly living in the will of God. This feels very ordinary and normal, sometimes even mundane, but it has incredible supernatural potential.

Let me give my definition of what the perfect will of God is…

**The perfect will of God is to receive the Father's love**

**and be transformed by it.**

That, right there, is the perfect will of God.

The perfect will of God is a wide and spacious place. When my kids are playing they are in the perfect will of their Mum and I. They're running around, jumping up on the trampoline, getting mucky, riding bikes, falling off, grazing their knees. They are enjoying each other and their surroundings, while, more than likely, squabbling with each other. It's all very normal. They're not paralysed from always trying to be perfect. Their parents are watching over them, seeing if there is real danger, but also allowing them to learn through risk-taking.

That's what our Father God does, as we grow in His love. He doesn't want us to be stunted or paralysed by saying, "This is My *perfect* will and that's not."

In many ways, His perfect will has a lot of flexibility in it because it is incarnated into the wiring of who we are as humans.

You can be guided in this way. You can begin to trust likes and dislikes. Because the resurrected life is incarnated in the human person.

The other thing is this: Our whole idea of what is 'perfect' is misguided anyway.

When the Bible uses the word 'perfect' it doesn't mean

'flawless.' It means 'complete.'

You see, we are so deceived by religion but we are also deceived by the deeply ingrained culture we have been born into. Greek mindsets are a big problem. Western Christianity has been influenced massively by Greek philosophy. Someone said that the Christian church has been much more influenced by Plato than by Jesus. It is largely true.

To put it in a very simple way, the Greeks had a very strong belief in a concept of 'perfection.' Amazingly, the idea of 'perfection' is not in Hebrew thought at all, even in relation to God Himself. The Hebrews think about everything relationally whereas the Greeks are always thinking about 'ideals' that have to be attained to. Biblical mindsets are not focused on perfection or ideals. We have projected this onto our reading of the Bible.

The other thing the Greeks believed is that the physical body was inferior to the mind. So the body was a prison, or, alternatively, there was an idolatry of the body so to attain to the ideal of the body, you had to spend a lot of time at the gymnasium. Sounds familiar!

Physical development and prowess, for the Greeks, was an attempt to escape base humanness. They saw human nature as degraded and humiliating. That's not the way the Bible sees things, either in the Old or New Testaments.

Christianity is incarnational. God wants to come down

and be enveloped by flesh. He wants to move into and live within the human body. We are fully human and fully earthed and in some ways, one with creation. A true son or a true daughter is not someone who is so heavenly minded that they are no earthly good. A real Christian is a doorway between heaven and earth.

The Father has no problem with us experimenting. He loves to see it.

I love to see my children trying to do things, growing a little bit more, climbing a little bit higher. I take them to a climbing wall and they get geared up in all the equipment and each time we go they venture a little bit higher, take more of a risk.

Father God is the same with us. He loves us to begin to experiment with the will of God to see what happens when we take a risk. It brings a wide grin to His face to see us pushing the boundaries.

# CHAPTER 17

# THE KINGDOM OF THE BELOVED

God has given His kingdom to His Beloved.

The person who is God's chosen King is the Beloved One.

The only people who can bring in the Kingdom are those who are in the Beloved.

There is no other alternative.

I used to think I was bringing in the Kingdom by shouting loudly, stomping around, binding this and that. I saw a lot happen actually, but I missed the essence of the Kingdom. The true Kingdom, the true dominion, is held in the heart of the one who is *deeply loved*.

The power of the Kingdom is not separate from the love of the Father. The Kingdom is the dominion of the Father's love.

Without love there is no real power.

When you surrender to divine love you will begin

to see the Kingdom come because it is a kingdom, a *dominion,* of love.

All of creation will align itself with love.

Paul, the apostle, got this. He prays:

> *May you be strengthened with all power, according to His glorious might, for all endurance and patience with joy, giving thanks to the Father, who has qualified you to share in the inheritance of the saints in light.*
> — COLOSSIANS 1:11,12

*You* are qualified!

You are qualified *by the Father* to share in the inheritance of the saints in light.

Then he says:

> *He has delivered us from the domain of darkness and transferred us to the Kingdom of His beloved Son, in whom we have redemption, the forgiveness of sins.*
> — COLOSSIANS 1:13,14

The 'domain of darkness' is not just the occult. It's not just horrible demonic stuff. That's one end of the continuum.

The domain of darkness is a state of being where there is a lack of revelation.

When you begin to see that you are not an orphan and the Father loves you, you are coming out of the domain of darkness into light.

When you begin to realise that you *do deserve* the love of God you are coming out of the domain of darkness into light.

When you realise that God has chosen you to co-participate with Him and with Christ in His great work of pouring love throughout the cosmos, you are coming into light.

What is more, the Father has delivered us from the domain of darkness and transferred us to the Kingdom of the *Son of His love.*

I spent a lot of my life focused on the 'Kingdom of God.'

Kingdom this, Kingdom that, trying to wield authority, shouting and commanding, "…in the *name* of *Jesus.*" I even adopted a different tone of voice as if that made any difference.

Let me tell you this:

The King, *God's* king, is His *Beloved.*

God's anointed king *is a son.*

I thought I was doing the work of the Kingdom but, for me, it was about power not love.

But God's chosen sovereign, God's appointed king, his

vice-regent, the person who governs on His behalf *is the one who lives in love.*

Brennan Manning said this, "Define yourself as one who is radically loved by God."

There *isn't* a Kingdom of power and authority without love,

…and Love has a very different authority than what I thought it did.

I've often wondered how Jesus cast demons out of people; it doesn't tell you in detail how He did it.

Did He shout or did He just look at the person with the eyes of love?

Maybe it was simply His presence.

Maybe, when He looked at them, they knew they eternally belonged and found their true identity, and the demonic grip slid off them.

Jesus operated in the Kingdom. He operated in total love.

I'm reminded of John G. Lake who said that he saw a time coming when there will be a move of the Spirit in gentleness, tenderness and love beyond anything our minds have ever conceived of, when the sons of light will meet the sons of darkness and prevail. You see, the kingdom is a dominion of love, through the masculine and the feminine2. It is direct *and* nurturing; the pointed arrow and the sharp sword *as well as* the womb and the surrounding arms.

You don't have to hype it up to have authority. When Jesus raised Lazarus from the dead He was moved by *compassion*. According to John's Gospel, He wept three times, that was the motivation He moved in miraculous power with. A few years ago I prophesied to a very gentle lady, "There's a calling of the supernatural on your life, but you don't have to be roaring and raving authority up the front. That is not who you are. You can follow the pathway of compassion into the power of the supernatural." Her eyes were opened to see possibilities she had never considered before.

As Jesus did at the tomb of Lazarus, you can go down that selfsame pathway of compassion and it will take you into the supernatural. If you're not a prophetic, cutting edge sort of person, it doesn't matter. Just follow your own individual inclination. Remember, it can be for an animal or even a plant. If you have compassion for something in creation, allow your compassion to flow and anointing will flow along the pathway of your compassion.

The other day I was in the bathroom and a hornet or wasp came flying in. In my old way of doing things I would have puffed out my chest and commanded it angrily, "In Jesus' name, get out!" But, do you know what I said? I said

---

2. See Genesis 1:26-28.

in peace and gentleness, "There's nothing for you in here. Whatever you want is not in this little enclosed bathroom, so you can just leave." And the thing just flew out. You see, kingdom authority comes in peace and love.

# CHAPTER 18

# ETERNAL INCARNATION

The sons and daughters of God carry an earthly chromosome and a heavenly chromosome.

Jesus carried a heavenly chromosome but He was still His mother's child. In many ways it's the same with us.

Yes, He is unique.

But not as far removed from us as we assumed.

We are human and earthly, and we too have spiritual and heavenly DNA from our Father.

God is extremely pleased to indwell the human condition. God is even pleased to indwell the *fallen* human condition because everybody in the Bible that He ever came into was fallen.

Apart from Jesus, it goes without saying.

The person who first incarnated God fully was Mary.

She literally and physically conceived, was pregnant with, and gave birth to, the Son.

So far, so good.

But hold on! Wasn't she a normal human being?

Was she not fallen like the rest of the human race?

The Roman Catholic Church could not handle this insult to religious intelligence. How could this supremely holy God come and begin His earthly life in a normal woman?

They could not swallow the fact that Mary was an ordinary person in sin, who carried the Son of God in her womb and He had some of her chromosomes, yet He was without sin.

(Don't misunderstand me. There is a lot to admire about the Catholic culture. Protestantism has thrown out the baby with the bathwater).

So they came up with the doctrine of the Immaculate Conception.

The Immaculate Conception is not actually about Jesus. Some people believe it is about Jesus being born without sin but no, the Immaculate Conception is the doctrine that *Mary*, His mother, was born without sin.

The reason why the Roman Catholic Church probably came up with that (and I'm not criticising, I'm just saying) is because people have found it very difficult to swallow the fact that God would actually incarnate Himself in a normal human person.

They couldn't handle it because of their Greek thinking, so they had to make up the fact that Mary was actually conceived without sin, but that's not true. Mary was a normal person but she incarnated and carried in her womb the Son of God.

We need to make a big breakthrough in our theology because we've got to wake up to the fact that all of us are the temple of the Living God. Jesus is not absent, He is present.

What is more, the Trinity is here right now, within you and I.

The Incarnation is here to stay.

If you can begin to believe that in your heart it will be extremely transformative for you. If you can believe that in all of your mess, you are still carrying around God — Father, Son and Holy Spirit — you will move in an authority you never thought possible.

Father is pleased to come down and indwell His human temple.

Sonship is not going to lift you up out of your humanness.

Sonship is creating a vessel in you that His Holy Spirit can overshadow and Christ will be brought forth within you.

God is looking for people.

He saw this little girl Mary. Who knows what was in

her heart to qualify her to become the mother of God Incarnate?

God saw something in Mary and the Holy Spirit was happy to come and overshadow her. The Father was happy to come and put His seed into the womb of Mary.

Today, the same thing needs to happen. In the Spirit we need to again give birth to Christ upon the earth.

We need to become pregnant with the spirit of Christ, the spirit of the Father.

Father is wanting to come to us normal, little, broken, failing, weak human beings and say that in the New Covenant we are all worthy to be overshadowed by the Holy Spirit.

Can you accept that in your heart?

Can you have a heart open enough?

A heart receptive to have the seed of the Father put into you which will grow and manifest Christ through you.

Can you say, with Mary, *Let it be to me according to Your Word.*

I am beginning to believe that I am the temple of the living God.

I'm believing it at a heart level, at a cellular level.

I'm believing that I'm carrying Father, Son and Holy Spirit, the most blessed Holy Trinity, within myself.

I want to impart it into you.

That you will come to believe at a heart level that you are the temple of the Living God.

That we are the Ark of the New Covenant.

That Christ in you is the hope of glory.

# CHAPTER 19

# YOU ARE A SEED OF SOMETHING WONDERFUL

I really love this Mexican proverb:

*"They tried to bury us. They didn't know we were seeds."*

Do you identify with that? Has that been your experience? It has certainly been mine. It is all too common in the orphan system.

You may feel 'buried' right now.

But have you ever considered that you are a seed? That you contain hidden life which will never die and whose germination will flourish in future centuries or millennia?

Have you considered that you are a seed of some plant that will grow in resurrection life beyond your lifetime?

Has anyone tried to bury you? Do you fear being lost in obscurity and submerged in the seeming insignificance of a mundane life?

Do you realise that you are a seed?

An embryo is hidden in secret before it is given birth to. If we have an eternal perspective, we will see that it may be over the course of a number of lifetimes that our 'ministry' will come into effect. What you are sowing now may not even be reaped in your own lifetime. Here's a thought to ponder; maybe you are not sowing as much as you are *being sown*.

Maybe your life is about the formation of a seed. After all, Jesus said that His Father was the gardener (John 15:1).

I like to think that we are the seeds of God's planting, and that He is sowing us into a cosmic soil, and one day we will appear as flowers and plants.

We often focus on our own span of years, thinking that *we* are responsible for what we achieve here on earth during our lifetime. What if it's a lot more than that? What if you are being sown by the Father into the rich loam of Spirit and the impact of who *you* are as a child of God is beyond your wildest imagination?

A seed has massive generative potential within it. You can create a forest of a million trees from that one seed. Yet this will still not exhaust the generative power of that seed.

Our lives are being sown as a seed into an eternal soil. When we have this perspective it takes away a lot of the striving to make an impact in this life. A seed is not 'productive' but it is 'fruitful.' Productivity is something that we strive after in this life but fruitfulness is something that is eternal, springing from the hidden depths and the hidden 'death' of a tiny seed in the earth.

Paul the apostle said that if there is no resurrection of the dead, then we are of all men the most miserable, and that our faith is futile (1 Corinthians 15:12-19). Christianity can only really be experienced on resurrection ground, beyond the death of something.

All life in the cosmos is seed-life. In Genesis 1:12, God sowed seed and every seed brought forth fruit *according to its kind.* In 1 Corinthians 15: 35-49, Paul points out that we humans are also seeds who are sown by God into a deep soil, in order that fruit *according to the kind of the seed* will, in future, spring forth. What is sown will spring up. But sowing involves a burial in darkness. Seeds are comfortable with being sown. Seeds do not resist being sown into the moist earth, to lie dormant for a while until the Spring comes.

Contemporary Christianity has lost the idea of being 'from generation to generation.' In orphanness there is no generation; no continuity from the past through the present to the future.

But you are not alone. You are not the beginning nor the end. You are part of a family whose Father is the Creator of the Universe, beyond your years, beyond time and space.

# CHAPTER 20

# WHAT IF...?

What if you lived a life without any fear whatsoever, and you just went and did what was on your heart? What if you were so without fear that you just did the first thing that you wanted to do? What if you were down to your last $50 and you really wanted to give it to someone, and you joyfully did that because you were fully confident that it would be remunerated to you.

If you had no fear of ever going without, you would have freedom to be abundantly generous to others. If you had no fear you would not need to live within the limitations. The whole world system, including the religious world system, lives within the limitations of the orphan-mind rather than the expanses of the heart and spirit.

The only limitations in sonship are the limitations imposed by love. Love places limitations on children to ensure their safety so that they will have access to a greater freedom as they grow. The strictures of the moral law, according to Galatians, are for those who are immature in love. Sons who are more mature in love can trust that love itself goes over and above the regulations, because love has its own inbuilt sense of responsibility.

I want to call upon the Holy Spirit to help us receive this. To release our imaginations and break us out of the box of our limited thinking. I'm asking the Holy Spirit to help you imagine that you are living right now in the New Creation.

That you have come to a place where you are completely free from all doubt, from all condemnation, where you have broken out of every box, where you are totally loved by Father and totally united with Christ.

Imagine that you are right now living totally at one with Christ in the perfect will of God.

When you begin to go there you then say, '*Well, what do I do with my life?*' You can do *whatever you like*, because you are one with Christ, because your desires have become His desires.

You will be totally motivated by love. Your enemies will not be enemies.

What if you were completely free from all of those burdens of second-guessing yourself, of comparing yourself, of doubting yourself?

What if we are totally new creations, what if we're in heaven *now*?

Let's break open the box of our imagination and believe

we are sitting in heaven.

What happens now if you believe you're totally united with Christ?

We can begin to engage with what's out there, whatever it is.

We can go out and say,

"Hello Creation! Have you been waiting for us? Well, here we are!"

What if you were totally free and God said, "Okay, it's time for you to go out and meet Creation. She's been waiting for you for a long time."

What skill are you going to use to heal her?

Are you going to dance her free?

Maybe you're going to write a letter or a poem to her.

Will you engage with her through art?

Will you use your voice to bring healing to Creation? Will you speak a prophetic word to her?

Will you use your body to embrace her, will you put your hand upon her? It's up to you because you are one with Christ. You are the Beloved.

I'm taking us into a place beyond condemnation. What is within you that you can engage with and say to Creation,

"I can see who you really are, come forth"

You are going to do something different than me.

Maybe you'll make Creation a cup of tea.

Maybe you'll hold Creation for a while till she calms down.

I'm just taking us to a heavenly place here. I am using this sort of language to stimulate our Spirit-fired imaginations.

Creation *will* respond to the voice of sonship.

When Jesus spoke to the wind and the waves and commanded them to be still, He actually used the word that a man would use if his dog was barking; "Quiet!"

"Be muzzled!" is how it reads in the original language.

That was what Jesus did when He calmed the wind and the waves.

He had this quality of relationship with Creation.

I want to open you up to who you really are, the highest point of God's creation, co-heirs with Christ in the Kingdom, through love and through weakness.

Not through some sort of a big heavy anointing thing.

Anointing comes out through who we are in ourselves; it's very gentle and very easy.

It's not about coming up to the front of a meeting and getting fired up.

I'm not in ministry to fire anyone up. I'm burnt out on being fired up!

So I want to call you forth very gently.

Call you into who you really are.

See yourself as one radically loved, radically chosen for partnership with the Trinity.

Believe, beyond all wavering doubt, that you are one who fully deserves the love of God.

You are one to whom the Father *wants* to give His Kingdom.

Father desires to love you and to live through you.

You are the zenith of all His hopes and dreams.

You can never earn His love or merit it.

But, praise God, you deserve it.

You deserve the love of God.

# OTHER TITLES BY STEPHEN HILL

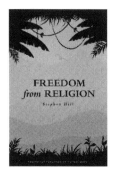

## FREEDOM FROM RELIGION

Available at:
**www.ancientfuture.co.nz**

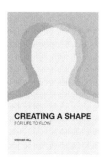

## CREATING A SHAPE
*For Life to Flow*

Available at:
**www.ancientfuture.co.nz**

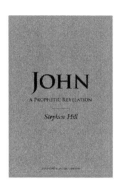

## JOHN
*A Prophetic Revelation*

Available at:
**www.ancientfuture.co.nz**

# OTHER TITLES BY STEPHEN HILL

## OUR TRUE IDENTITY

Available at:
**www.ancientfuture.co.nz**

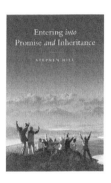

## ENTERING INTO PROMISE AND INHERITANCE

Available at:
**www.ancientfuture.co.nz**

Printed in Great Britain
by Amazon